Date: 3/30/16

J 797.1224 RIN
Ringstad, Arnold,
Kayaking /

Kayaking

BY ARNOLD RINGSTAD

Published by The Child's World®
1980 Lookout Drive • Mankato, MN 56003-1705
800-599-READ • www.childsworld.com

Acknowledgments
The Child's World®: Mary Berendes, Publishing Director
Red Line Editorial: Editorial direction
The Design Lab: Design
Amnet: Production

Photographs ©: Vereshchagin Dmitry/Shutterstock Images, cover
(top), 1 (top), 6; LUGO/iStockphoto, cover (center), 1 (center);
PhotoDisc, cover (bottom), 1 (bottom); Iasha/Shutterstock Images,
back cover (left), 3, 16; Creatas/Thinkstock, back cover (right);
Annal A/Shutterstock Images, back cover (bottom); Adam Silver/
Thinkstock, 4–5; Shutterstock Images, 7, 12, 18; iStockphoto,
8, 14, 15; DigitalVision 10; Stephanie Corbel/Thinkstock, 11;
Thinkstock, 13, 17, 20–21; Graham Heywood/iStockphoto, 19

ISBN 9781626873322
LCCN 2014930669

Printed in the United States of America
Mankato, MN
July, 2014
PA02222

ABOUT THE AUTHOR

*Arnold Ringstad lives in
Minnesota. He would love to
kayak on the Mississippi River.*

CONTENTS

FUN WITH KAYAKING

Kayaking is an exciting way to explore nature. There are many places to kayak. You can tumble through a rushing river. You can glide

Kayakers enjoy beautiful scenery.

across a calm lake. Or you can kayak through a city.

You can kayak alone or with other people. You can even race against other kayakers. Kayakers enjoy the outdoors. They also get great exercise. Kayaking is an exciting and fun way to be outdoors.

WHAT IS KAYAKING?

Kayaking is the activity of using a kayak. Kayaks are small boats usually built for one or two people. Some kayaks look like **canoes**. Riders use **paddles** to move both kinds of boats through the water. But there are important differences. Kayak paddles have two **blades**. Canoe paddles have only one. Kayakers sit in their boats with their legs in front of them. Their legs are often inside their boats. Canoeists sit on seats.

The native people of the North American Arctic used the first kayaks. They built them from wood or whalebone. People used the boats for hunting. Kayaks move quietly through calm waters. The boats made it

This kayak is built for two paddlers.

easy for hunters to sneak up on animals.

Europeans have paddled kayaks since the 1800s. They used them for adventure and for hunting. Kayakers explored rushing rivers and waterfalls. Kayaking events were added to the Olympic Games in the early 1900s. They are still included in the Olympics today.

KAYAKS AT WAR
The quiet movement of kayaks has been useful in war. In World War II (1939–1945), some British soldiers used kayaks to sneak into enemy areas.

Kayaking can be a competitive sport.

PLACES TO KAYAK

People kayak all over the world. Kayakers can explore wherever there is water. The world's oceans contain many kayaking sites. Some sites are cold, while others are warm. Kayakers visit the bays and islands on the coast of Alaska. These are great places to paddle in the chilly North Pacific Ocean. Warmer waters can be found in Mexico and Thailand.

People enjoy kayaking along Alaska's coast.

Kayakers paddle in all sorts of freshwater, too. Those interested in rushing rivers visit the Salmon River in Idaho. The Upano River in Ecuador is another popular location. Parts of the Upano River are gentle. Others are very rough. In one of the river's **gorges**, kayakers are surrounded by pounding waterfalls.

Kayakers explore more than just the wilderness. Many cities are located along rivers or shorelines. The Tennessee River is popular with kayakers. They paddle beneath the bridges of Chattanooga, Tennessee. Boston and Washington, D.C., give kayakers a chance to see historic sites from the water.

LONG-DISTANCE KAYAKING

People can kayak for amazing distances. A woman named Helen Skelton kayaked more than 2,000 miles (3,200 km). She traveled down the Amazon River in South America.

WHITE WATER KAYAKING

White water is river water that runs quickly over rocky riverbeds. When water travels over rocks, it splashes and bubbles. It looks white in color. That is where white water gets its name. Traveling on white water rivers can be dangerous in large boats. Experienced kayakers use special kayaks to safely **navigate** white water.

Many rivers have white water.

White water kayaks have special shapes. They are short and have rounded bottoms. They are usually up to 9 feet (2.7 m) long. This makes it easier for kayakers to turn quickly. It helps them steer around sharp rocks. Rocks and crashing water can damage kayaks. White water boats must be built with strong materials.

Kayakers sit inside white water kayaks. Their legs are inside the boat. Only their upper bodies stick out. They use their upper bodies to help power their paddling. They must also keep their balance. If they don't, their kayak may tip over into the water.

SEA KAYAKING

Sea kayakers usually paddle in calmer waters than white water kayakers do. The early native people who invented kayaking were sea kayakers. The smooth, quiet motion of their boats made it easier to hunt animals. Today, sea kayakers like this quietness. It lets them enjoy nature.

Like white water kayaks, sea kayaks have special shapes. Sea kayaks are usually longer and wider than white water boats. They have flat bottoms. They have sharper angles on their sides. These features make sea kayaks move smoothly and quickly. They keep the boat going in a straight line. But they also make sea kayaks more difficult to turn than white water boats.

Sea kayaks have sharp angles on their sides.

Some sea kayaks are designed to have the rider sit inside. Others let the rider sit on top. Some sea kayaks may have a **rudder**. A rudder helps the kayaker steer the boat. Some boats have space for gear, such as a water bottle, sunscreen, and a towel.

People sit on top of these sea kayaks.

CHOOSING A KAYAK

The most important piece of equipment for kayakers is the boat itself. White water and sea kayaks have different shapes. But there are other differences among kayaks. Boats are made of different materials. Some materials are stronger than others. Kayakers must decide what kind of kayak will work best for their needs.

Kayaks are usually made of plastic. This makes them durable and cheap. But the plastic also makes them heavy. White water kayakers need to make quick turns. They prefer lightweight kayaks. **Fiberglass** and a material called **Kevlar** are light and strong. But they are much more expensive than plastic. Sea kayaks are

Kevlar kayaks are light and strong, but expensive.

usually made of plastic, too. However, some are wooden instead.

Many kayaks include **compartments** for storage. Kayakers who travel into the wilderness can store food, dry clothes, or even a tent for camping. Kayakers planning short trips may not need much storage.

Some people go camping when they kayak.

MOVING THROUGH THE WATER

After the kayak, the most important piece of gear is the paddle. Kayakers cannot push forward or steer around rocks without a paddle. All kayak paddles have a blade on each end. Paddles with wide blades push kayakers through the water faster. But kayakers need more strength to use them. Narrow blades are easier to paddle with. But the kayak will not move as fast.

Kayakers can also choose feathered or unfeathered blades. Unfeathered blades face the same direction. Feathered ones tilt in different directions. Feathered blades help stop the wind from slowing kayakers down. When one blade is in

Kayak paddles have two blades.

the water, the other blade is angled into the wind. This lets the wind move over the blade more easily. Kayakers do not have to fight the wind as they paddle.

Paddles come in many different materials. Like kayaks, they can be made from plastic, fiberglass, Kevlar, and wood. Some are also made from metal.

KAYAKING SAFETY

Kayaking is exciting. But it can also be dangerous. Kayakers use special gear to keep them safe. They take courses to learn kayaking skills.

Life jackets and helmets are two important pieces of safety gear. Kayakers know their boats may tip over. A life jacket could save a kayaker from drowning. Kayakers use special life jackets. They are different than those for other kinds of water activities. They have wide neck

LEARNING TO PADDLE

Kayaks can be very difficult for beginners. It takes practice to learn how to stay upright. It also takes time to learn how to paddle in a straight line. Many people take kayaking classes to learn these skills.

This kayaker is wearing his safety gear.

holes and arm holes. This makes it easier for
kayakers to move their bodies while paddling.
Helmets protect kayakers from the sharp
rocks found in white water rivers.

Some kayakers sit with their legs inside their
kayaks. They can become trapped underwater
if their boats flip over. Kayakers learn rolling
skills to flip the kayak back up. Most use their
paddles to push themselves back up. Rolling
can be difficult to learn. But the skill can save a
kayaker's life.

Rolling a kayak is difficult to master.

MANY KINDS OF FUN

Kayaking is a sport with many choices. Kayakers can explore rivers and oceans all over the world. They can move through rushing rivers, calm seas, or busy cities. They can race, hunt, or simply enjoy the scenery.

Kayaking is a sport that's fun for many people.

People can kayak by themselves or with a friend. Kayakers can choose from different shapes and materials for kayaks and paddles.

Some kayakers travel through the wilderness for days in small kayaks. They carry camping gear and explore rivers and lakes. Others may kayak for an afternoon on a city lake. The many options available to kayakers make it a great sport for anyone to try.

GLOSSARY

blades (blaydz): Blades are the wide parts at the end of paddles. Blades let the kayaker push the kayak through the water.

canoes (kan-OOZ): Canoes are long, narrow boats. Canoes and kayaks have several different features.

compartments (com-PART-ments): Compartments are parts of a kayak where items are stored. Kayakers store camping gear in compartments.

fiberglass (FYE-bur-glass): Fiberglass is a light, strong material. Some kayaks and paddles are made from fiberglass.

gorges (GORJ-ez): Gorges are narrow valleys with rocky walls. Rivers and streams sometimes run through gorges.

Kevlar (KEV-lar): Kevlar is a light, strong material that is very expensive. Some fancy kayaks are made from Kevlar.

navigate (NAV-eh-gayt): To navigate is to carefully move through water. White water kayaks navigate easily through rough water.

paddles (PAD-ulz): Paddles are equipment used to push kayaks through the water. Paddles come in many different materials.

rudder (RUD-ur): A rudder is a part of a boat used for steering. A sea kayak may have a rudder.

white water (WITE WAW-tur): White water is quickly moving water in a river that looks white as it passes over rocks. Some people like to canoe in white water.

TO LEARN MORE

BOOKS

De Medeiros, James. *Kayaking*. New York: AV2 by Weigl, 2013.

Harasymiw, Raymond. *Kayaking and Rafting*.
New York: Gareth Stevens, 2013.

Hardyman, Robyn. *Kayaking and Canoeing*.
New York: Windmill Books, 2014.

WEB SITES

Visit our Web site for links about kayaking:
childsworld.com/links

Note to Parents, Teachers, and Librarians: We routinely verify our Web links to make
sure they are safe and active sites. So encourage your readers to check them out!

INDEX